*For the first time
I have received the Host.
It is the Body of Jesus.
And I drank from the chalice.
It is the Blood of Jesus.*

*The risen Jesus
lives within me.
He and I are one.*

*I say "Thank You"
for the greatest gift
God has given me.*

People who came to my First Communion

My First Communion

Remembrance Book

by Nadia Bonaldo

Pauline
BOOKS & MEDIA

Boston

Nihil Obstat:
 Very Rev. Timothy J. Shea, V.F.

Imprimatur:
 ✢ Bernard Cardinal Law
 September 21, 1993

Illustrated by Carla Cortesi

Artwork by N. Musio: pages 31, 35, 43, 45, 47, 51, 53, 76–77

Photo Credits: Mary Emmanuel Alves, FSP, pp. 17, 37, 39, 41, 49, 55, 63, 67, 69, 73, 81, 97, 103; FSP/USA Photo Archives, p. 89; Barbara Gerace, FSP, p. 19; PhotoDisc®, pp. 24–25, 105; Armanda Santos, FSP, pp. 91, 95

Cover: Regina Frances Dick, FSP

Scripture quotations are from the *Holy Bible: Contemporary English Version.* Copyright © American Bible Society 1995. Used by permission.

English translation of the *Doxology* and *The Apostles' Creed* by the International Consultation on English Texts.

Original title: La mia prima Communione; Un giorno da ricordare. Copyright © 1991, Figlie di San Paolo, Milan, Italy.

Translated from the Italian by Janet and Frank Alampi

ISBN 0-8198-4824-7

Printed and published in the U.S.A. by Pauline Books & Media, 50 Saint Pauls Avenue, Boston, MA 02130-3491.

www.pauline.org

Pauline Books & Media is the publishing house of the Daughters of St. Paul, an international congregation of women religious serving the Church with the communications media.

1 2 3 4 5 6   08 07 06 05 04 03

Contents

This Is How I Began

My Adventure as a Child of God

A Small Seed...

When I was very small, my parents, godparents and
many relatives and friends brought me to church.

I was baptized there.

I could not walk so they carried me.

I could not understand or talk.

So they understood and talked for me.

That day I became a child of God.
I became a member of a great family: the Church.

My parents and godparents made a promise to God and the Church.
They promised to help me live and grow as a child of God.

Photograph
of my
Baptism

I was baptized at _____ *Parish*

on (date) _____ .

I was given the name _____ ,

which means _____

_____ .

The name of the priest (or other minister) who baptized me is

_____ .

My godparents are _____

_____ .

God, our Father,
*   with Baptism*
*   you have freed us from sin.*
You have called us into your Church.
You have made us your children.
The Spirit of Jesus
*   lives in our hearts.*

...Grows So Slowly

This year I will be _____ years old.
I'm growing up.
There are always new things to learn.

I know now that at home I can't always say
"I want, I want."
I learn to think of how others feel.
Sometimes my daddy worries.
My mom works hard.
My little brother or sister wants to play.
I learn to think of them, too.

At school I can't only think of doing better
than the others.

Sometimes one of my friends is by himself.
Sometimes another friend doesn't have
a snack.
I learn to be kind to them.

I play with my friends.
I learn to take turns choosing games to play.
I learn not to be bossy.
I learn to share toys, even new ones.

This year Jesus is asking more of me.
He invites me to become his good friend.
He wants me to be very close to him.

Jesus says:
"I am the true vine, and my Father is the gardener....
Stay joined to me and I will stay joined to you.
Just as a branch cannot produce fruit
unless it stays joined to the vine,
you cannot produce fruit
unless you stay joined to me.
I am the vine,
and you are the branches.
If you stay joined to me, and I stay joined to you,
then you will produce lots of fruit.
But you cannot do anything without me."

—*John 15:1, 4–5*

16

An Important Choice

My parents and I have accepted Jesus' invitation. It was an important decision.

I don't understand everything that "making First Communion" means. But I know two things for sure:

- I keep the promise my parents and godparents made for me when I was baptized.
- I answer Jesus' invitation to be his friend. He asks me to love just as he loves.

For now, I tell Jesus that I'm happy to know him better.
I'm happy to listen to his Word and to do what he tells me.

I can use this prayer:

I thank you, Lord, because you teach me your way.
"Obeying your instructions
brings as much happiness as being rich.
I will study your teachings
and follow your footsteps….
Your teachings are wonderful,
and I respect them all.
Understanding your word
brings light to the minds of ordinary people."
—*Psalm 119:14-15, 129-130*

The Signs
of God's Love

*A Rainbow…
to Remember*

I have learned many beautiful things during these months.

I have learned that God loves us very much.

God has always tried to be our friend.

Many, many years ago…

Again God said to Noah and his sons:
"I am going to make
a solemn promise to you
and to everyone who will live
after you....
I promise every living creature
that the earth and those living
on it will never again
be destroyed by a flood....
When I send clouds
over the earth,
and a rainbow
appears in the sky,
I will remember
my promise to you
and to all other living creatures."

—*Genesis 9:8–9, 11, 14–15*

Every time we see a rainbow in the sky
we can remember that God has promised
us his love and care!

25

An Adventure...

God has not only spoken through nature.
He came to his people wherever they were.
When people suffered God proved he was
their friend.

This is how things happened many years
later.

The Israelites were the people God loved in
a special way.
The Israelites were slaves of the Egyptians.
The Egyptians forced the Israelites to do
very hard work.
The Israelites prayed to God, the friend of
their fathers.
They asked God to help them.

And so God decided to free his people.

He planned to bring them to a rich and
fertile land.

God called Moses to be the leader of the
Israelites.
God split the water of the Red Sea so that
Moses could lead the people through on
dry land.
It was a real miracle!
When the Egyptian army tried to chase the
Israelites through the Red Sea, the water
came back down on them.

The Israelites were free!

To celebrate their escape from Egypt,
Moses and the Israelites sang this song
to God:

"I sing praises to the Lord
 for his great victory!
He has thrown the horses
and their riders into the sea.
The Lord is my strength,
 the reason for my song,
  because he has saved me.
I praise and honor the Lord—
 he is my God and the God of
  my ancestors....
Our LORD, no other gods compare
 with you—
Majestic and holy!
Fearsome and glorious!
Miracle Worker!...
Our LORD, you will rule forever!"

     —*Exodus 15:1–2, 11, 18*

27

A Lamb to Celebrate Freedom

We like to remember wonderful adventures.
We especially like it when we are with friends.

The Israelite people could not forget how they were freed from slavery in Egypt.
They wanted to remember what God had done for them.
So every year the Israelites ate a lamb, thin bread made without yeast, and bitter herbs.

This is how they celebrated the Passover Feast.

God himself told them to do this:
"Remember this day and
*   celebrate it each year*
*   as a festival in my honor....*
Celebrate this Festival of
Thin Bread as a way of remembering
the day that I brought your families
and tribes out of Egypt."

—Exodus 12:14, 17

Here are some of the words the people of Israel use
on the night of Passover.

They celebrate and thank God for creation,
freedom and the gift of his law.

*"Praise the L*ORD*! He is good.*
God's love never fails.
He lets the sun rule each day.
God's love never fails.
He lets the moon and the stars
rule each night.
God's love never fails.
He rescued Israel from Egypt.
God's love never fails.
He split the Red Sea apart.
God's love never fails.
The Lord brought Israel safely
through the sea.
God's love never fails.
The Lord led his people
through the desert.
God's love never fails.
He rescued us from our enemies.
God's love never fails.
Praise God in heaven!
God's love never fails."

—Psalm 136:1, 8–9, 11, 13–14,
16, 24, 26

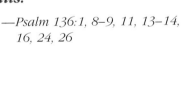

But Jesus Is
the Greatest Gift!

Later the people forgot all that God had done for them.
They still did not love one another.

God sent a gift that was much more important than the rainbow.
This gift was much greater than freedom from Egypt.
God gave us himself.
God gave us his Son Jesus whom he loves very much.

It is important to know the life of Jesus.
It is important to learn about his words, his miracles, his death and
resurrection.
If we want to know God, we must look at Jesus.

Jesus has freed us from sin.
He helps us love each other as brothers and sisters.
His name, "Jesus," means "God Saves."
God could not give us a greater gift!

Jesus
the Son of God and Friend of All

The Words of Jesus

Jesus lived in Nazareth, a small village in Galilee. He worked as a carpenter like his legal father, Joseph. When Jesus was about thirty years old, he left his home and his work. He said good-bye to Mary his mother. He went from town to town. He had to tell everyone that God is our good Father. Jesus told us that we must love one another. Jesus wants us to be one, as he and the Father are.

Jesus walked along the dusty roads of Palestine. He spoke to the young and old. He spoke to people who lived good lives and to people who didn't. All the people were speechless as they listened to him. His words were not hard to understand. Everyone understood because Jesus' words touched their hearts.

One day Jesus climbed a high mountain.

He spoke to the people. He said:
"God blesses those who put their trust in him.
God blesses those who are sad.
God blesses those who are not violent.
God blesses those who are kind to others.
God blesses those who are pure of heart.
God blesses those who are peacemakers.
God blesses those who suffer for doing what is right.
Be joyful and happy because God has prepared a great reward for you!"

—See Matthew 5:1–12

Jesus said,
*"Let the children come to me,
and don't try to stop them!
People who are like these children
belong to God's kingdom."*

—Matthew 19:14

Jesus Also Said...

"Look at the birds in the sky!
They don't plant or harvest.
They don't even store grain in barns.
Yet your Father in heaven takes care of them.
Aren't you worth more than birds?

"Why worry about clothes?
Look how the wild flowers grow.
They don't work hard to make their
clothes.
"But I tell you that Solomon with all his
wealth wasn't as well clothed
as one of them....
"Your Father in heaven knows that you
need all of these. But more than anything
else, put God's work first and do what he
wants. Then all other things will be yours
as well."

—Matthew 6:26, 28–29, 32–33

"I am giving you a new command.
You must love each other,
just as I have loved you.
If you love each other,
everyone will know that you are my disciples."

—John 13:34–35

"Treat others as you want them to treat you."
—Matthew 7:12

*"I tell you for certain that the Father will give
you whatever you ask for in my name."*
—John 16:23

*"I will be with you always,
even until the end of the world."*
—Matthew 28:20

The Parables of Jesus

To tell everyone that God is our good Father, Jesus used parables. Parables are stories. Jesus used stories from the everyday life of the people of his time.

The parable of the lost sheep

Everyone loved Jesus very much. But there were also people who complained about Jesus. They complained about him because he spent time with sinners. Jesus knew very well what these complainers thought. One day he said to them:

"If one of you has a hundred sheep and loses one, what does he do? He leaves the ninety-nine safely in a sheep pen. Then he goes to look for the one that is lost until he finds it.
When he finds it, he is very happy. He puts it on his shoulder and returns home.

'Come to my house, come and we will celebrate,' he shouts to his friends and neighbors. 'I have found the sheep that was lost!'"

At the end of the story Jesus said:

"God loves each one of us just like that shepherd. He knows each one of us. He takes care of us. He has no peace if even one is lost. I tell you that in heaven there is more happiness over one sinner who comes back to God than over the ninety-nine good people who don't need to."

—See Luke 15:1–7

Jesus also told us:
"I am the good shepherd.
I know my sheep
and they know me...
I give up my life
for my sheep.."

—John 10:14–15

The Miracles of Jesus

Jesus didn't only tell beautiful stories and show love to everyone.
He also worked many miracles. This is how he showed his power.

Jesus heals a little girl

One day, Jesus was walking. A man named Jairus fell at Jesus' feet.
He was the leader of the synagogue (the place where the Jewish
people went to pray). Jairus begged Jesus to go to his house. Jairus'
only child, who was about twelve years old, was dying.

As they were going toward the house, Jairus' servant came
toward them. He said, "Your daughter is dead. Don't bother the
Master any more."

But Jesus said to the leader of the synagogue, "Don't be afraid. Only
trust and your daughter will be saved."

When Jesus reached Jairus' house, he found a great crowd of
relatives and friends. They were all crying. When he heard all the
noise, Jesus said, "Why are you crying and making all this noise?
The child is not dead but asleep."

But no one believed him. They laughed at him. So Jesus called
the girl's parents and Peter, James and John. They went into the
child's room with Jesus. Jesus knelt near her bed. He held the girl's
hand. It was cold. Jesus said to her, "Little girl, get up!"

The little girl opened her eyes. Then she smiled and got up.
Next Jesus told her parents to give her something to eat. He said
not to let anyone know what had happened.

—See Luke 8:40–56

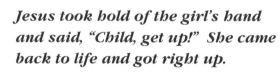

*Jesus took hold of the girl's hand
and said, "Child, get up!" She came
back to life and got right up.*

—Luke 8:54–55

The multiplication of the loaves and fishes

That day many people followed Jesus into a valley. The valley was far away from the people's homes. No one even noticed that night was coming. The disciples were worried. When Jesus stopped speaking, they said to him, "This is a deserted place. Let the people go. They need to get something to eat before it gets dark."

Jesus answered, "Why don't you give them something to eat?"

The disciples were surprised. They looked at one another. Even King Herod's treasure would not be enough to feed all those people!

Then Andrew, Peter's brother, said jokingly, "There is a little boy here. He has five loaves of barley bread and two fish.... We can give a crumb to each person!..."

"Tell the people to sit down on the grass," Jesus told the disciples.

They saw that he was not joking.

Jesus took the five loaves and two fish. He said the blessing. Then he broke them and gave them to his disciples. They gave the food to the people. On that day all the people ate until they were satisfied.

—See John 6:1–15

43

The Living Bread

The next day the crowd that followed Jesus was even bigger. They thought that after his speech there would be another free meal.

But Jesus said, "You look for me because you have eaten the bread. But I will not give you anything to eat except myself. I am the living bread that comes from heaven. I am the bread that gives life. Those who believe in me will not be hungry any more. Those who trust me will not be thirsty any more."

They all looked at one another in surprise. "What is he saying? Has the sun gotten to him? Has he gone crazy during the night? Maybe we haven't really understood him!"

Jesus said, "If you do not eat my body and drink my blood, you will not have life in you! Those who eat my flesh and drink my blood are one with me and I with them. They will live forever."

"Now he is making this up! Who can listen to things like this? How can he give us his body to eat?" And even those who had been following Jesus for a long time went away.

Only his twelve apostles stayed. They were hurt and disappointed.

"Do you want to leave, too?" Jesus asked. He looked into their eyes.

But Peter said, "Lord, to whom shall we go? Only you speak the words that give eternal life!"

So the twelve apostles stayed with him.

—See John 6:22–68

Jesus then asked his twelve disciples if they were going to leave him. Simon Peter answered, "Lord, there is no one else that we can go to! Your words give eternal life."

—John 6:67–68

45

The Last Supper
Explains Everything

The feast of Passover was near. On this day, the Israelites celebrated their freedom from slavery in Egypt. They renewed their promise to love and obey God. Jerusalem was full of people. They came from all over.

Jesus' closest followers, the apostles, also prepared everything for the feast. There was a lamb, some wine and some bread. Jesus knew that this would be his last supper with his friends.

During the supper Jesus took the bread. He broke it and gave it to his friends. He said, "Take this. It is my body which is given for you." And he gave it to them to eat.

Next he took the cup of wine. He said, "This is my blood given for you. Do this in memory of me." Then he gave it to them to drink.

Now they understood better what Jesus had told them about the living bread.

Jesus loves us so much that he gave his life for us.

Jesus Loved His Friends to the End

Jesus' Passover meal with his friends was over. They went to a garden called Gethsemane. It was close by and Jesus often rested there with his disciples.

Things started to happen very quickly. The garden was suddenly filled with noises. Lanterns shone in the darkness. Men carrying weapons came toward Jesus. For a long time they had waited to capture him and put him to death. The moment had arrived. On Friday Jesus was nailed to the cross and died. His disciples were sad and confused.

They did not understand that Jesus died to give us life. They did not understand that he would rise. They were afraid. So much had happened in such a short time! They locked themselves in a house. All day Saturday they stayed there. They cried for Jesus, their friend who had died.

"The greatest way to show love for friends
is to give your life for them," Jesus had said.

The life of Jesus was like bread.
He gave it to all those whom he met.
He had "broken" himself for everyone.
He never thought of himself.

The life of Jesus was also like wine.
He "poured" himself out for everyone.
He never thought of himself.

Jesus Is Alive!

On Sunday morning Mary of Magdala went to the tomb where they had put Jesus' body. Some other women went with her. They brought perfumes to anoint Jesus' body.

This was a Jewish custom. The women did not speak along the way. They were worried. They wondered who would move the large stone in front of the tomb for them.

But when they arrived, the tomb was open. The rock was rolled far away. They saw that something special had happened.

When they went into the tomb, two men in shining white robes suddenly stood by them. They said, "Why do you look here for someone who is no longer dead? Jesus is not here. He is risen, he is alive!"

The women left the tomb in a hurry. They were both afraid and happy. They ran to tell the disciples, "Jesus is risen!"

—*See Luke 24:1–12*

Forever with Us

That day, Jesus himself appeared to the disciples. At first they thought he was a ghost. They had locked the door of the room where they were hiding because they were afraid. How could a living person get in?

"Peace be with you!" Jesus said. "Do not be afraid. Touch me and look at me. It is really I. A ghost cannot have flesh and bones like I do!"

Jesus' friends were happy to see him. And Jesus said again, "Peace be with you. As the Father has sent me, so I send you." He breathed on them. Then he said, "Receive the Holy Spirit."

Now it was as if the disciples had a fire inside their hearts. The risen Jesus had given them his Spirit. They would never be alone.

53

Sunday: the Day of the Risen Lord

The disciples often talked about the day they had met the risen Jesus. They said, "It was on the day of the Lord."
They called that day "Sunday."

So each Sunday the disciples would come together to "break bread and drink from the same cup." The Mass soon became the center of life for the first Christians.

When they ate the bread and drank from the cup, they became one with the risen Jesus. Jesus' friends were changed from frightened people into brave men and women. They faced suffering without fear. They began their journeys to the corners of the earth.

**Sunday is a special day for us, too.
Today the place where we go to pray is different.
The songs and the language are different, too.
But we, too, receive the Body and Blood of Jesus.
We meet the risen Jesus.
It is just as if we were with him on the shore of Lake Galilee.**

The Liturgy
of My First Communion

A Special Sunday

Today is not a Sunday like all the others. Today something important happens for me. It is the day of my First Communion Mass. We are leaving our house. All of my family is happy with me. They have come to celebrate my first meeting with Jesus.

I come to you, Jesus,
   with a heart full of love.
I come to you, Jesus,
   to learn how to live and act as you did.
I come to you, Jesus,
   as your child.
I come to you, Jesus,
   to learn to grow as you grew.
I come to you, Jesus,
   with all my dreams.
I come to you, Jesus,
   to pray for my parents, relatives and friends.
I come to you, Jesus,
   to give you all that I am.
I come to you, Jesus,
   to thank you for giving yourself to me!

We come to you, O Lord, with hearts full of joy.

Photo of my family
on the day of my
First Communion

I put a photo of my
family here

We Come with Joy to Your House

I meet all my friends at church. We have prepared for this important day. There is my religion teacher. There are flowers, music and great joy. We are all ready to meet Jesus our special friend. He is a friend who will never leave us.

We have all answered Jesus' invitation. He wants us to be with him.

We are happy. Our hearts are glad.
Today we come into your house.
At your table you gather us, Father.
We are your children.
Christ loves us, Christ invites us.
His Word is our only light.
Our life has been lit
like the sun lights the sky.
We celebrate at home with our friends.
One Bread unites us all.
The risen Christ is alive and with us.
He will be our friend.
God's Church, sing with us.
This is the day the Lord has made.

—A.M. Galliano, I Come to You

Forgive Us, Lord

At the beginning of Mass the priest invites us to be silent. He invites us to ask pardon for all our sins. It's a little hard. I feel very excited. I know that this moment is important. I want to be able to welcome Jesus with a loving heart. I think of what I have done during the week.

—I made up excuses for not helping my mother.
—I made believe I didn't hear what my grandfather asked me.

Lord, have mercy.

—I was unkind to my classmates.
—I told a lie.

Christ, have mercy.

—I didn't do my chores.
—I fought with my brother and sister.

Lord, have mercy.

The priest prays. We pray with him that God may have mercy on us. We ask God to forgive us our sins. We ask him to bring us to heaven with him.

It's wonderful to have a friend like you, Jesus.
You always forgive us. You never get tired of loving us, because you are Love.

Glory to God

You have forgiven us, Lord.
We have many reasons for praising you today.
Glory to you, God the Father.
You are good, you love us.
We all sing, young and old.
We are one voice.
One family.
We feel like your children.

Holy Father, Creator of the world,
*   you rule the heavens and the earth.*
We ask that your kingdom come,
*   that your will be done.*

Jesus Christ, Lamb of God,
you take away the sins of the world.
You sit at the right hand of the Father.
Listen to our prayer.

Glory to you, Holy Spirit,
*   who unite the Church in one body.*
You spread your gifts all over the world.
You are a fountain of life and love.

Glory to God
and peace to God's people.
We adore you.
We give you thanks.
We praise you, Lord.

Speak, Lord, We Are Listening

Everyone is quiet at the next part of the Mass because now the Lord will speak to us. We don't see him. But he speaks through the voice of the person who reads from the big book of the Word of God.

Jesus also speaks today, just as he spoke a long time ago to the people in Palestine.

The Word of God is like a seed.
Our heart is the ground where it's planted.

Lord, for many, many years
   your Word has been read all over the world.
   Your Word is always true!
Lord, your Word is a light for us.
   It tells us all you have done.
   It's like a lamp on our path.
Lord, your Word is not just any word.
   It is very special.
   Help me to do what your Word tells me.

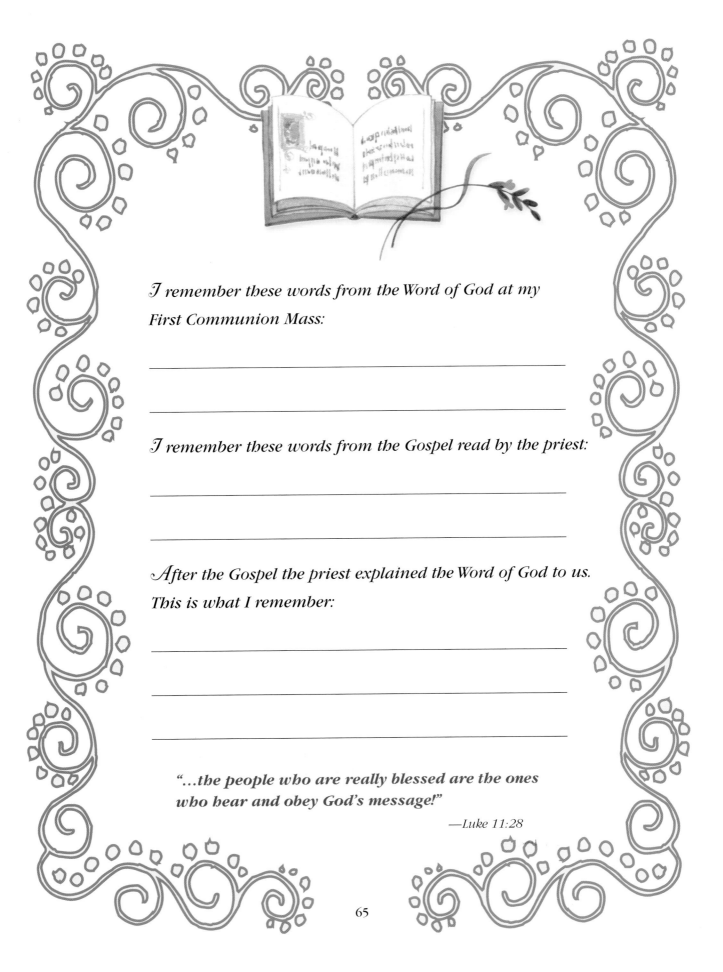

I remember these words from the Word of God at my First Communion Mass:

_____

_____

I remember these words from the Gospel read by the priest:

_____

_____

After the Gospel the priest explained the Word of God to us. This is what I remember:

_____

_____

_____

"...the people who are really blessed are the ones who hear and obey God's message!"

—*Luke 11:28*

65

We Believe

We have listened to the Word of the Lord.

The priest has helped us to understand it.

May it grow and bloom just like the seed planted in good soil.

Now we are all invited to say what we believe.

We say a prayer called the Creed.

In many countries people can't talk about their faith in you, God.

So I say with all my strength that I believe in you.

I believe that you love us.

I believe in one God,
 the Father,
 Creator of heaven and earth.
I believe in Jesus Christ,
 the only Son of God,
 who died and is risen for us.
I believe in the Holy Spirit,
 the Lord, the giver of life.

This is our faith.
This is the faith of the Church.

Hear Us, O Lord

We really feel like brothers and sisters.
We are children of the same Father.
We are one family: the Church.

As in every family, each one has his or her duty.
Each person is important.
If one person suffers, the others are also less happy.
If one person is happy, the others are all happy, too.

This is how it is in the Church.
Now we pray for the needs of all people everywhere.

Let's pray!

> —*for the Church, the Pope, the bishops*
> —*for priests, religious, missionaries*
> —*for our families, for our religion teachers*
> —*for the people who make our laws*
> —*for everyone who takes care of us*
> —*for children, for young and older adults*
> —*for those who are alone, who are poor or sick*
> —*for the hungry and for those in prison*

Lord, hear our prayer.

Jesus Took the Bread and Wine...

Now as then

We all sit down. Now the Liturgy of the Eucharist begins.
The priest takes the bread and wine. He puts them on the altar.

There is a beautiful white tablecloth.
It's like the one my mother uses for special occasions.
We are also preparing a feast. A very special feast.

The bread we eat and the wine we drink feed us in a very
special way. The priest thanks the Lord for these gifts.

Blessed are you, O Lord, who have created all things.
You have given us this bread that we offer to you.
It will become the bread of life for us.

Blessed be God forever.

We thank you also for this wine,
made of many grapes.
It will become our spiritual drink.

Blessed be God forever.

This bread is made of a thousand grains of wheat
that have been ground up and kneaded.

This wine is made up of many grapes.
When we offer the bread and wine,
we also offer ourselves to God our Father.

We offer you, good Father,
*   our desire to play, to jump and run.*
And today we also offer our desire
*   to be good friends of Jesus.*
May we always walk with him.

We offer you, good Father,
*   the pains of those who suffer.*
We offer you the worries of those
*   who have many problems.*
We offer you the desires and hopes
*   of each person's heart.*

Jesus Offered Thanks...

Now as then

Everything is ready on the altar. It has become a beautiful table.
The church is like the room where Jesus ate the Last Supper with
his friends. Jesus is risen from the dead. He is alive!

By the power of the Holy Spirit, the bread and wine will become
Jesus' Body and Blood. Now as then, Jesus gives his life for us.

The priest repeats the words and actions of Jesus. We pay attention
to what he is saying and doing.

O God our Father,
   you have brought us together again.
   We are here to say "thank you."
   We want to sing your praise.
We praise you for all the great and wonderful
   things you have made.
We thank you for the joy you put in our heart.
   We bless you for the sun
   which gives light to the day.
We bless you for your Word,
   which is light for our mind.
We thank you for the fields,
   for the oceans and the mountains.
We thank you for the people who live on earth.
We thank you for the life you have given us.
For all these wonderful gifts of your love
   we sing your praise!
Heaven and earth are full of your glory.
   Praise to you!

We Thank God the Father for the Gift of Jesus

Good Father, you always watch over us.
*   You never forget anyone.*
To free us from sin you sent your Son Jesus,
*   our Savior.*

He lived with us and did good to everyone.
He healed the sick. He gave sight to the blind.
He pardoned sinners. He welcomed children
*   and blessed them.*

O Father, in Jesus we see your great love
*   for everyone!*
And now we show our joy in song.

Blessed is he who comes
in the name of the Lord.
Praise to you!

One People

Good Father,
    we offer you our praise.
We praise you with your Church all over the world.
We praise you with our Pope and our bishop.
Together with your Mother Mary,
    with the apostles,
    with the angels and all the saints,
    we sing the hymn
    of your glory.

Holy, holy, holy, Lord…
Praise to you!

Holy Father,
    to show our thanks
    we have brought the
    bread and wine to the altar.

        Send your Holy Spirit upon these gifts,
            that they may become
            Jesus' Body and Blood.
        In this way we can offer you
            what you have given us as a gift.
        A gift of your love.

75

Do This in Memory of Me

At the Last Supper with
his disciples,
Jesus took the bread.
He gave thanks.
He broke it and gave it
to his disciples.
He said:

**Take this all of you and eat it.
This is my body which will be
given for you.**

In the same way, he took
the cup of wine.
He gave thanks. He gave it
to his disciples and said:

**Take this all of you
and drink from it.
This is the cup of my blood.**

**It is the blood of the new and
everlasting covenant.**

My blood will be shed for you and for everyone so that sins may be forgiven.

Then he said to them:
Do this in memory of me.

We Offer the Father the Most Pleasing Gift: the Life of Jesus

There is silence while the priest prays. We all know something special is happening. Once again, at this very moment, Jesus gives his life to God the Father for all of us.

Now, Father,
  we do what Jesus has told us.
We offer you the bread of life.
We offer you the cup of salvation.
We proclaim Jesus' death and resurrection.

Jesus, you gave your life for me.
I too can offer my life to the Father, every day.
  I can offer it with you.

I offer my wish to play.
I offer my wish to learn new things. I offer:

_____

_____

_____

_____

Christ has died for us.
Christ is risen for us.
Come, Lord Jesus.

We Pray for the Whole World

Father, you love us so much.
You let us receive
 the Body and Blood of Jesus.
All together in the joy
 of the Holy Spirit,
 may we be one family.

Look with kindness on our parents,
 our brothers and sisters,
 and our friends,
 on those who work,
 on those who suffer,
 on us who are here,
 and on all the people of the world.

Lord, welcome into the joy of heaven
 those who have died.

   O Father,
    we will always praise
    and thank you for your great
    love.

Through Christ,
with Christ,
in Christ,

in the unity of the Holy Spirit,
all glory is yours, O Father,
forever and ever.

Amen.

80

Father of All

The Bread and Wine are now the living Jesus.
He is here with us as he promised during the Last Supper.
This Bread and this Wine make us all brothers and sisters.
We are children of the same Father.

With joy we say:

**Our Father, who art in heaven,
hallowed be thy name;**

> *O God may all people
> know that you are Father.*

**thy kingdom come;
thy will be done
on earth as it is in heaven.**

> *Your kingdom has come with Jesus.
> He has brought us peace, brotherhood and truth.
> But you ask each of us to help make the world
> a better place.*

**Give us this day
our daily bread;**

> *Everything is a gift from you, Father.
> I offer you my hands and my heart.
> Jesus is our bread, because Jesus is life.*

**and forgive us
our trespasses.**

*You never stop loving us, Father.
Each time you forgive us,
you give us even more love.*

**As we forgive those
who trespass against us;**

*Jesus, teach us to forgive as you forgive us.
I need to know how to forgive
so I can be your friend.*

**and lead us not
into temptation,**

*May we not give in to temptation.
Lead us. Help us be strong so we can be good.*

but deliver us from evil.

*Free us from war and selfishness.
Give us real peace. So we can all live happily
in the wonderful world you have created for us.*

The Peace of the Lord Be with You

The risen Jesus gave a great gift to his disciples.
He gave them his peace.
Now the priest offers us the same peace. He says:

**The peace of the Lord
be with you always.**

We shake hands with those on our right and left.
I want to give a sign of peace to my whole family
and to the whole world.
I want everyone to share the peace of the risen Jesus.

**Peace be with you, my sister.
Peace be with you, my brother.
Peace be with all people.**

Jesus says:

"I am giving you a new command. You must love each other, just as I have loved you. If you love each other, everyone will know that you are my disciples.

I give you peace, the kind of peace that only I can give. It isn't like the peace that this world can give. So don't be worried or afraid."

—*John 13:34–35, 14:27*

The Blood of Christ. Amen!

This Wine which we drink
began as a root in the earth.

Then it became…clusters of grapes.
The grapes were picked and crushed to make wine.

Jesus, this Wine was made by many people with love.

Now it is your Blood, Lord Jesus,
and we receive
this wonderful Wine from you.

Jesus, may your Spirit
join our hearts as one.
May we live in joy.

Thank you, Jesus!

—*Based on* One Fine Day *by A. M. Galliano*

My First Communion

I eat the Bread.
I drink the Wine.

The life of Jesus becomes my life.
The Bread becomes my blood, skin, heart, energy,
strength, and courage.

It is the life of the risen Jesus.

> *Lord Jesus,*
>   *I believe you are the living Bread.*
>   *Only you give me joy and peace.*

Photograph
of my
First Communion

We have received the Body of Jesus.

Everyone around us is quiet.

Each of us is thinking about God being with us.

He is living and strong, hidden in that small piece of bread.

This is what I said to Jesus when I made my First Communion:

_____

_____

_____

_____

Your Body will always be
    the Bread that gives me strength.
Your Body will make my steps safe.

Your Blood will always be
    the Wine that takes away my thirst.
Your Blood will give me the courage
    to follow you.

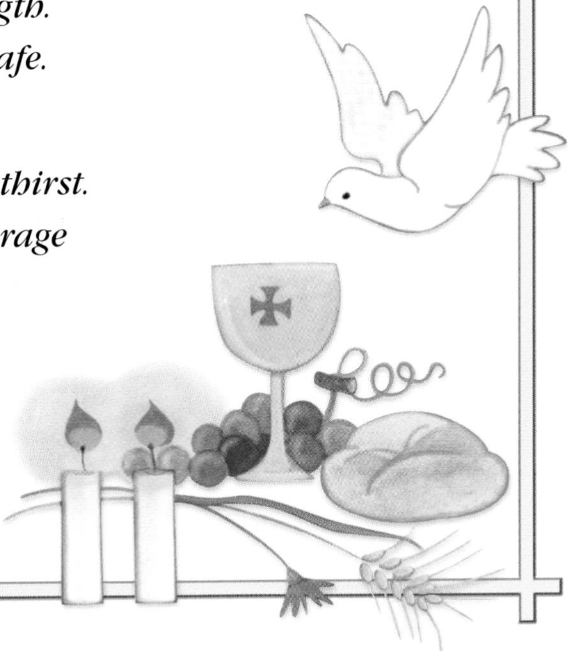

Let Us Go in Peace

It's time to say good-bye.
The Lord gives us another gift: his blessing.
He is saying to each of us,
"Go in peace. I am always with you!"

Go in peace

does not only mean that we may now go home.
No, it means that in all we do, we bring Jesus to others.

Every time I eat his Bread which gives life,
Jesus makes me more like himself!

Lord, make me an instrument of your peace.

Where there is hatred, let me bring love.

Where there is injury, let me bring pardon.

Where there is doubt, let me bring faith.

Where there is despair, let me bring hope.

Where there is darkness, let me bring light.

Where there is sadness, let me bring joy.

—St. Francis of Assisi

We Remain in Love

My friends,
    may the Lord's celebration
    never end for you.

Remain in love
and God will be with you.

My friends,
    may the Lord's joy
    shine in you.

Remain in love
and God will be with you.

My friends,
    may the Lord's grace
    be with you.
May he bring you every good thing.

Remain in love
and God will be with you.

My friends,
    may the Lord's strength
    guide your steps.

Remain in love
and God will be with you.

—A.M. Galliano, I Come to You

"God is love. If we keep on loving others, we will stay one in our hearts with God, and he will stay one with us."

—*1 John 4:16*

I put a photo of
my family here

I put a photo of
my family here

I put a photo of
my family here

A Celebration
without End

A New Strength

Many days have passed since my First Communion Mass.
Nothing seems to have changed. I still go to school.
I do my homework. I play. I still fight sometimes with my sisters
and brothers. My father and mother still work as they did before.

But everything is the same only on the *outside*.
Inside me there is a new strength.
It is the strength of the Lord Jesus.

His Spirit reminds us of what he said:

**"You must love each other.... If you love each
other, everyone will know that you are my
disciples."**

—John 13:34–35

It is not easy, Jesus, to love as you love.
But you promised not to leave us alone.
You will always be with us.

One day you will return.
Then we will see you
   face to face.

Meanwhile,
   you want us
   to love each other.
You want us
   to prepare for our most important
   meeting with you.

I Look Around and See You Present

I see you, Lord Jesus,
in the love of my mother and
father.
I see you in the patience of my
grandparents.
I see you in the friendship of my
friends.

I see you, Lord Jesus,
in all the people who work
to make things better in our
world.
I see you in the people who help
the elderly, the sick,
the handicapped.

I see you, Lord Jesus,
in that family helping
a young person addicted to
drugs.
I see you also in that family
that has adopted another child.

I see you present, Lord Jesus,
in the priests, religious and
missionaries.
I see you in all those people who
help others.

Your rainbow makes our lives
beautiful.
It is with us today.
Those who see it know that you
love us.

I Can Also Help

Jesus, I want to help other people to know you.
I want them to know you are close to them.

I can help my father and mother
*   by showing my love for them.*
I can help my teacher by obeying.
I can help my friends to love one another more.
I can help them welcome new friends.
I can help other people to smile.

Jesus, I am only a child.
But you need me, too,
*   to build a more beautiful world.*
I could not do much by myself.
But with you I can.

I go to Mass each week
*   to listen to you, to become one with you,*
*   and to bring you to others.*

These are some ways I will help others:

_____

_____

_____

_____

_____

_____

_____

My **Weekly Eucharist**

The church where I go to Mass is called

_____ .

The children's Mass is at _____ .

I go to Mass with

_____ .

The part of Mass I like most is

_____ .

The most beautiful words I hear during Mass are

_____

_____ .

Some words that are hard for me to understand are

_____

_____ .

"Your kindness and love will always be with me each day of my life, and I will live forever in your house, Lord."

—*Psalm 23:6*

My Prayers

The Sign of the Cross

In the name of the Father, and of the Son, and of the Holy Spirit. Amen.

Our Father

Our Father, who art in heaven, hallowed be thy name. Thy kingdom come. Thy will be done on earth as it is in heaven. Give us this day our daily bread, and forgive us our trespasses, as we forgive those who trespass against us. And lead us not into temptation; but deliver us from evil. Amen.

Hail Mary

Hail Mary, full of grace, the Lord is with you. Blessed are you among women and blessed is the fruit of your womb, Jesus. Holy Mary, Mother of God, pray for us sinners, now and at the hour of our death. Amen.

Glory

Glory to the Father, and to the Son, and to the Holy Spirit: as it was in the beginning, is now, and will be for ever. Amen.

The Apostles' Creed

I believe in God, the Father almighty,
creator of heaven and earth.
I believe in Jesus Christ, his only Son, our Lord.
He was conceived by the power of the Holy Spirit
and born of the Virgin Mary.

He suffered under Pontius Pilate,
was crucified, died and was buried.
He descended to the dead.
On the third day he rose again.
He ascended into heaven,
and is seated at the right hand of the Father.
He will come again to judge the living and the dead.
I believe in the Holy Spirit,
the holy catholic Church,
the communion of saints,
the forgiveness of sins,
the resurrection of the body,
and the life everlasting. Amen.

Hail, Holy Queen

Hail, holy Queen, Mother of Mercy, our life, our sweetness, and our hope. To you do we cry, poor banished children of Eve; to you do we send up our sighs, mourning and weeping in this valley of tears. Turn then, most gracious advocate, your eyes of mercy toward us, and after this our exile, show unto us the blessed fruit of your womb, Jesus. O clement, O loving, O sweet Virgin Mary.

Angel of God

Angel of God, my guardian dear,
to whom God's love entrusts me here,
ever this day be at my side to light and guard,
to rule and guide. Amen.

A Prayer to Jesus in the Holy Eucharist

*J*esus, even though I cannot see you, I know and believe that you are here in the Holy Eucharist. I know that you watch over me. I know that you listen to all my prayers. I can tell you everything because you are my very best Friend!

Please take care of my parents and family, Jesus. Please help all people who are suffering. Please help all people who are sick or have problems. Please let everyone in the world live in love and peace. Amen.

A Thank You Prayer

(You may use this prayer to thank Jesus for coming to you in Holy Communion.)

*T*hank you for coming into my heart, Jesus. I love you! I want to become more and more like you every day. I want everyone to know and love you, too.

Here are some special things I want to pray for…
(Now tell Jesus whatever is in your heart.)

Thank you for everything, Jesus! It will be wonderful to receive you in Holy Communion again. Amen.

A Prayer of Sorrow

*H*ave mercy on me, God, because you love me. Sometimes I do things that are wrong. But I know that you will always forgive me when I am sorry. Please wipe away all my sins. Give me a new heart that is full of love for you. Help me to be strong and good. Amen.

—Based on Psalm 51

The Rosary

The rosary is a special prayer. It helps us remember the lives of Jesus and Mary. While we think about Jesus and Mary, we pray the *Our Father,* the *Hail Mary* and the *Glory.* We use a chain of beads called *rosary beads.* The *mysteries* of the rosary are different events that we remember in the lives of Jesus and Mary

The chart on the next page will show you how to pray the rosary. Before you start, tell Jesus and Mary about the people you want to pray for. Talk to them about your needs or problems. Thank them for all they do for you. Here are the mysteries of the rosary:

The Joyful Mysteries

1. **The Annunciation**—*The angel announces to Mary that God has chosen her to be the mother of his Son. Mary says yes.*
2. **The Visitation**—*Mary visits her cousin Elizabeth*
3. **The Nativity**—*Jesus is born*
4. **The Presentation**—*Mary and Joseph present Jesus to the Lord in the Temple*
5. **The Finding in the Temple**—*Mary and Joseph find Jesus in the Temple*

The Mysteries of Light

1. **Jesus is Baptized in the Jordan**—*John baptizes Jesus*
2. **Jesus Works His First Miracle at Cana**—*Jesus changes water into wine at the wedding feast*
3. **Jesus Proclaims the Kingdom of God**—*Jesus teaches the people about God's kingdom*
4. **The Transfiguration**—*Jesus shines with the light of God's glory*
5. **The Institution of the Eucharist**—*Jesus gives us his Body and Blood under the signs of bread and wine*

The Sorrowful Mysteries

1. **The Agony in the Garden**—*Jesus prays and suffers in the garden*
2. **The Scourging at the Pillar**—*The soldiers whip Jesus*
3. **The Crowning with Thorns**—*The soldiers put a crown of thorns on Jesus' head*

4. ***The Carrying of the Cross***—*Jesus carries the cross to Golgotha*

5. ***The Crucifixion***—*Jesus is nailed to the cross and dies for our sins*

The Glorious Mysteries

1. ***The Resurrection***—*Jesus rises from the dead*

2. ***The Ascension***—*Jesus goes up to heaven*

3. ***The Descent of the Holy Spirit***—*Jesus sends down his Holy Spirit upon Mary and the apostles*

4. ***The Assumption***—*Mary is taken body and soul up to heaven*

5. ***The Coronation***—*Jesus crowns Mary Queen of heaven and earth*

18. Pray the *Hail Mary* on each of the following ten beads.

6. Pray the *Hail Mary* on each of the following ten beads.

19. Pray the *Glory* after the last *Hail Mary*.

17. 5th Mystery. Pray the *Our Father.*

7. Pray the *Glory* after the last *Hail Mary*.

16. Pray the *Glory* after the last *Hail Mary.*

20. End here. Pray the *Hail, Holy Queen.*

5. 1st Mystery. Pray the *Our Father.*

15. Pray the *Hail Mary* on each of the following ten beads.

4. Pray the *Glory.*

8. 2nd Mystery. Pray the *Our Father.*

3. Pray *Hail Marys* on these three beads.

2. Pray the *Our Father.*

9. Pray the *Hail Mary* on each of the following ten beads.

14. 4th Mystery. Pray the *Our Father.*

1. Start here. Make *The Sign of the Cross.* Pray the *Apostles Creed.*

10. Pray the *Glory* after the last *Hail Mary.*

13. Pray the *Glory* after the last *Hail Mary.*

11. 3rd Mystery. Pray the *Our Father.*

12. Pray the *Hail Mary* on each of the following ten beads.

Pauline
BOOKS & MEDIA

The Daughters of St. Paul operate book and media centers at the following addresses. Visit, call or write the one nearest you today, or find us on the World Wide Web, www.pauline.org

CALIFORNIA
3908 Sepulveda Blvd, Culver City, CA 90230   310-397-8676
5945 Balboa Avenue, San Diego, CA 92111   858-565-9181
46 Geary Street, San Francisco, CA 94108   415-781-5180

FLORIDA
145 S.W. 107th Avenue, Miami, FL 33174   305-559-6715

HAWAII
1143 Bishop Street, Honolulu, HI 96813   808-521-2731
Neighbor Islands call: 800-259-8463

ILLINOIS
172 North Michigan Avenue, Chicago, IL 60601   312-346-4228

LOUISIANA
4403 Veterans Memorial Blvd, Metairie, LA 70006   504-887-7631

MASSACHUSETTS
885 Providence Hwy, Dedham, MA 02026   781-326-5385

MISSOURI
9804 Watson Road, St. Louis, MO 63126   314-965-3512

NEW JERSEY
561 U.S. Route 1, Wick Plaza, Edison, NJ 08817   732-572-1200

NEW YORK
150 East 52nd Street, New York, NY 10022   212-754-1110
78 Fort Place, Staten Island, NY 10301   718-447-5071

PENNSYLVANIA
9171-A Roosevelt Blvd, Philadelphia, PA 19114   215-676-9494

SOUTH CAROLINA
243 King Street, Charleston, SC 29401   843-577-0175

TENNESSEE
4811 Poplar Avenue, Memphis, TN 38117   901-761-2987

TEXAS
114 Main Plaza, San Antonio, TX 78205   210-224-8101

VIRGINIA
1025 King Street, Alexandria, VA 22314   703-549-3806

CANADA
3022 Dufferin Street, Toronto, Ontario, Canada M6B 3T5   416-781-9131
1155 Yonge Street, Toronto, Ontario, Canada M4T 1W2   416-934-3440

¡También somos su fuente para libros, videos y música en español!